Evening and morning

by **Rachel Abel**

This short creation sketch works best with at least twelve children, or fewer children with adults for the speaking parts. You will need large cards with pictures of the main categories of the creation story, except vegetation which can be represented by fruit, flowers, and plants. Make sure the children are well-rehearsed to keep the sketch moving. As each child enters with their visual aid, they bow to the *Voice of God*. You might want to use background music for this sketch

---

Cast: **Voice of God, Chorus, Man, bearers of visual aids**

Voice: Let there be light!
(Enter child carrying card showing Light. The child bows before the Voice of God)

Chorus: And there was evening and there was morning, the first day.
(Exit Light)

Voice: Sky! Come from among the waters.
(Enter child carrying the card of Sky)

Chorus: And there was evening and there was morning, the second day.
(Exit Sky)

Voice: Waters! Come together and be called seas.
(Enter child carrying card of Sea)
Dry land! Come out and be called Earth. Bring out all sorts of trees, plants and fruits.
(Enter child representing Earth, with the fruit, flowers and plants)

Chorus: And there was evening, and there was morning, the third day.
(Exit Earth and Sea)

Voice: Lights! Separate the day from the night and be signs for spring, summer, autumn and winter for a very long time.
(Enter Light again, with two cards: day and night. The 'day' card can include illustrations for the different seasons)

Chorus: And there was evening, and there was morning, the fourth day.
(Exit Light)

Voice: Waters! I want you to bring forth lots of sea animals.
(Enter Sea again with another card filled with pictures of sea animals)
Birds! From this day, start flying above the earth across the heavens.
(Enter child with card of bird in flight)
Water animals and birds, I bless you. Begin to multiply.

Chorus: And there was evening, and there was morning, the fifth day.
(Exit Sea and Bird)

Voice: Earth! Now bring out cattle, dogs, lions, hens, cats, gorillas, tigers, cheetahs, reindeer, rabbits, elephants, butterflies, cockroaches, ants, spiders, and everything I have dreamed.
(Enter Earth again with colourful illustrations of these animals)
Now, it is time to make man.
(Enter a boy. He too bows)
Man, I give you power over every other thing I have made. Be blessed. Multiply, eat of every green plant and their fruit.
(Lays his hand on the child's head in an act of blessing)

Man: Thank you, dear Lord.

Chorus: And there was morning, and there was evening, the sixth day.
(Exit man)

Voice: I am glad to finish making everything in heaven and earth. They are very, very good. Now I can have some rest.
Seventh day!
(Enter a child with 'seventh day' pinned on his T-shirt. The Voice of God holds his hands)
I bless you. I make you a day of rest and holier than the others days that I used for my work.
(Exit child)

All the children come back together, holding their cards, props or hands high, and all say together:

God has now completed his work. Everything he has made is good indeed.

It works well to finish off the sketch by singing 'All things bright and beautiful'.

JON WEBSTER

JESUS – THE MAN AMONG US

Placing children at the heart of Jesus' adventures

Sixteen sessions with . . .

Stories

Drama

Discussion

Thoughts

Prayers

kevin
mayhew

First published in 2004 by

KEVIN MAYHEW LTD
Buxhall, Stowmarket, Suffolk, IP14 3BW
E-mail: info@kevinmayhewltd.com

9 8 7 6 5 4 3 2 1 0

ISBN 1 84417 280 5
Catalogue No. 1500716

Edited by Graham Harris
Cover design by Angela Selfe
Typesetting by Kevin Whomes

Printed and bound in Great Britain

Contents

Introduction

Drama can be a very powerful learning experience. I once took part in a Passion Parade as Second Roman Soldier, right in the centre of Long Eaton, Derbyshire. I will always remember the experience, made all the more poignant by the hailstorm, right on cue for the Crucifixion!

In my role as a teacher I meet many children who know virtually nothing about Jesus or what he said or did. This book is an attempt to present some of the main Gospel stories in a very accessible way, showing children that Jesus is a human and approachable figure, not someone whose life is frozen in a stained-glass window. It aims to put them right at the heart of the action, to experience it for themselves and to identify closely with the people in the stories.

The book is aimed at junior school age children in schools, church organisations or other young people's groups.

Each presentation has six sections:

1. The introduction (which can be read out loud to the group).
2. The story. This can be read out loud from the page or used as background information to enable you to tell the story in your own words in as animated a way as possible.
3. A script, which can be acted out as a drama or with puppets.
4. Discussion section, followed by . . .
5. . . . A brief, final thought.
6. A prayer.

The key is flexibility, so use the ideas and resources in your own way – you know the children in your group and what will work best with them.

There are no stage directions, as they can be muddling for young children. Use your own, but keep it simple! If you're concerned about children forgetting their lines or if you have never tried drama before, here are two simple ideas:

1. The whole class or group can say their lines and learn them together – that way they won't feel so self-conscious, and if anyone is absent on the day of the performance, you'll have plenty of understudies!
2. You can use readers to read out the lines offstage, while actors mime the action in view of the audience.

If you have time, get the children to draw and colour posters for the play before you perform it. Activities like this help to develop their sense of involvement and, even, their understanding of the story.

Above all, enjoy the experience – children learn so much better when they're having fun!

You can e-mail me at <puppets@education8.freeserve.co.uk> for advice, help and encouragement. Have fun!

Jon Webster

Picking a Team

Introduction

We all need friends, but we need good friends – friends who will help and support us. We don't need friends who will get us into trouble or run away and leave us when the going gets tough. We need to choose our friends carefully, and that's exactly what Jesus did.
He didn't choose friends who were rich or famous, or even clever. He was looking for people who would listen and learn and really help him – friends who could work together as a team and not fall out or argue.
So this is how he chose them.

Story

Jesus was wandering along the beach beside the lake one day, deep in thought. He needed friends – people he could trust. Then he saw some fishermen, pulling their nets into their boat – they looked really fed up!
'What's up, lads?' he called out to them.
'We've been out fishing all night!'
'Haven't you caught anything?'
'Nothing, mate,' they answered, looking really cheesed off.
Jesus thought for a moment, and then said: 'Try the other side!'
They stared at him.
'The other side of the boat – try the nets on that side!'
They looked at each other with raised eyebrows, as if to say: 'What does he know about fishing?'
Then one of them, a big fellow called Peter, said: 'Sure – we'll give it a go.'
And they did. They lifted the nets out of the water and dropped them on the other side of the boat. And suddenly the nets were full – to bursting point. The fish were fighting to get into them.
'Easy does it, lads,' said the big fellow. 'We don't want to tear the nets!'
Carefully they eased the catch into the boat, then sat looking at each other – and Jesus.
'You're that Jesus bloke, aren't you?' said one called Andrew.
'Yeah, you're the teacher,' said James. 'You tell people about God.'
'And heal sick folk,' said John. 'You're a bit of a local hero round here.'
'Anyway,' said Peter. 'Thanks for your help with the fish.'
'But I need your help now,' said Jesus. 'I need mates I can really trust – to help me teach people.'
They all looked puzzled and Peter scratched his head.

'You want us to help you?' he asked. 'We'd be no good – we can't read or write! We're just fishermen – you need folk who are clever – educated! None of us has been to school!'

Jesus looked at them for a moment.

'No,' he said calmly. 'I need you lot – you're a team! You work together! And I can trust you!'

They looked at each other. Then they looked at Peter – he was their leader. He nodded.

'OK, lads – we'll go with him. Let's pack away the nets!'

But Jesus shook his head.

'There's no time for that! We have to get started!'

'All right, boss, if you say so!' said Peter.

'Come on, lads!' said Jesus. 'Fishers . . . of people – that's what I'll make you!'

'Sounds fine to me,' said James.

And John added: 'We won't let you down!'

Then they followed Jesus without another word.

Drama script

Cast: Narrator, All, Jesus, Peter, Andrew, James, John.

Props (Optional): Make a boat out of chairs or an upturned table.

Get the children to mime pulling in the heavy nets of fish.

Narrator	Jesus was wandering along the beach one day, deep in thought. He needed . . .
All	Friends!
Narrator	But who could he really trust? Then he saw some fishermen pulling their nets into their boat. They looked really . . .
All	Cheesed off!
Jesus	What's up, lads?
Peter	We've been fishing all night.
Jesus	Not caught anything?
Peter	Nothing, mate!
Jesus	Try the other side!
Peter	Eh?
Jesus	Try the nets on the other side of the boat!
Narrator	The men looked at each other, as if to say . . .
All	What does he know about fishing?
Peter	OK, we'll give it a go.
Narrator	So they did. They lifted the nets out of the water . . .
All	Ooooh!

Narrator And dropped them on the other side of the boat. And suddenly . . .

All Look!

Narrator The nets were full of fish – to bursting point! The fish were fighting to get into them!

Peter Easy does it, lads. We don't want to tear the nets.

Narrator Carefully they eased the fish into the little boat. Then they looked at each other – and at Jesus!

Andrew Hey! It's that Jesus bloke!

James The one who tells people about God – the teacher!

John The one who heals sick folk!

Andrew Everyone knows him round here!

Peter Thanks, mate – we needed those fish!

Jesus That's OK, but now I need your help.

All Eh?

Jesus To help me teach people.

Narrator They looked puzzled. Peter scratched his head.

Peter You want us to help you?

Andrew We'd be no use.

James We can't read . . .

John . . . or write.

Andrew We're just fishermen.

John You need someone clever.

Jesus No, I need you – you're a team and I can trust you.

Narrator They looked at each other. Then they looked at Peter – he was their leader.

Peter Sounds fine to me – let's pack away the nets.

Jesus There's no time for that!

All Let's get started!

Peter OK, boss.

Jesus I know. I'll make you . . .

All . . . Fishers of people.

James We won't let you down, boss!

Narrator Then they followed him without another word.

Discussion

We all need friends, but what makes a good friend? Any ideas?

What kind of people can you really trust?

How should you treat a friend?

Final thought

Jesus was pretty good at choosing the right kind of friends. They needed to be the kind of people who wouldn't give up easily, or let him down when the going was tough. We need friends like that, too.

But don't forget the other side of the coin. We need to learn to be good friends, too. If we expect our friends to be loyal to us, then we must stick by them.

Prayer

Dear God,
Please help us to choose good friends . . . and help us to learn to be good friends.
For Jesus' sake,
Amen.

What a Storm!

Introduction

Jesus was a kind and caring man. His friends trusted him and knew he would never let them down. But Christians believe he was also God's Son and that he had amazing power to do good. His friends hadn't seen this side of Jesus until one day when they faced real danger.

Story

It's tiring being a teacher and Jesus often became exhausted. He needed some peace and quiet, so he liked to go out walking in the hills on his own.

It was so peaceful up there – he could really chill out! But one evening, after a long, busy day, he told his friends: 'Put the boat out, lads, we'll have a little sail on the lake – it'll be nice and quiet out there.'

'OK, boss,' said Peter. 'Pull up the anchor, lads.'

Off they sailed, and Jesus was right – it was peaceful on the lake.

'Time for a nap, lads,' said Jesus, and he grabbed a pillow and stretched out in the bows of the little fishing boat.

'He's got the right idea,' said Andrew.

His friends smiled – Jesus was already asleep.

But the peace was soon shattered.

'Look at those black clouds,' said Peter.

There were ripples already forming on the lake as the wind got up. Soon there were waves round the boat and it began to rock.

'Pull those ropes in, lads,' said Peter.

It only took a few minutes for a full-blown gale to set in. The waves were now battering the tiny craft.

'Lash those sails down,' yelled John. 'Make for shore!'

But it was no good – the storm was tossing the boat up and down. The wind was screaming – it was tearing the sails.

The fishermen had been in many storms, but they'd never seen anything like this before.

'We'll never make the shore!' cried James. 'The sails are in shreds!'

The boat was filling with water.

'Bail it out quickly!' called Peter.

But it was no good – they were on the point of sinking.

But where was Jesus?
Still fast asleep in the bows – as peaceful as a baby!
'Wake up, Jesus,' cried Andrew. 'You've got to help us – we're sinking!'
Jesus sat up and rubbed his eyes. He looked puzzled.
'Couldn't you trust me to look after you?' he muttered.
Then he stood up. He sounded a bit annoyed.
'Quiet! Enough!' he growled at the wind and the waves.
Now, you won't believe this, but the wind immediately began to die down and the waves got smaller. Everyone breathed a sigh of relief.
'Phew!' Peter wiped his brow. 'Now bail out the water, lads!'
In a few minutes it was calm again . . . but no one spoke. They all loved Jesus – he was their best mate. But a man who could calm a storm with one word? That was scary! They just looked at each other. And Jesus? He just settled back to sleep!
'Wake me up when we get to shore, lads!' he yawned.

Drama script

Cast: Narrator, Jesus, All, John, James, Andrew.

The actors will need to mime the increasing rocking motion of the boat and the growing panic of the fishermen. You can try 'building a boat' from chairs, but you may find this restricts the children's actions. If this happens, it might be better to do without it.
Try to make sure that Jesus' relaxed mood contrasts with the disciples' fear. Jesus needs to show quiet authority.
Sound effects can be produced by children off-stage.

Narrator	It's pretty hard work being a teacher.
All	Give us a break!
Narrator	Jesus often got tired out.
Jesus	I need a bit of peace and quiet, lads.
Narrator	He often went out walking on the hills on his own – to chill out.
Jesus	Mmm! It's great up here! So quiet!
Narrator	But one evening after a long, busy day, he just said . . .
Jesus	Put out the boat, lads. We'll have a little sail on the lake. It'll be nice and calm out there.
Peter	OK, boss . . . push the boat out, lads.
Narrator	It was peaceful on the lake – hardly a ripple.
Jesus	Time for a little kip, lads.
All	No problem.
Narrator	So Jesus grabbed a pillow and was soon stretched out in the bows.

John	Beautiful evening.
James	Look at Jesus – he's off already.
Narrator	But the peace was soon shattered.
Peter	Hello . . . look at those black clouds coming this way.
Narrator	At first there were just little ripples and waves around the boat.
Andrew	Wind's getting up.
Narrator	Soon the boat was beginning to rock.
Peter	Pull those ropes in, lads.
Narrator	It only took a few minutes for a real gale to blow up. The waves were battering the little craft!
John	Lash those sails down!
James	Make for shore!
Narrator	But it was no good – the waves were tossing the little boat about like nobody's business.
Andrew	I've never seen anything like it!
Narrator	The wind was screaming and tearing the sails.
James	We'll never make the shore!
John	The sails are in shreds!
Andrew	The boat's filling with water!
Peter	Bail it out!
Narrator	But it was no good.
All	We're sinking!
Narrator	But where was Jesus?
All	Asleep!
Narrator	Yes, He was asleep in the bows – as peaceful as a baby!
Peter	Wake up, boss!
Andrew	You've got to help us!
All	We're sinking!
Narrator	Jesus sat up and rubbed his eyes. He looked puzzled.
Jesus	Couldn't you trust me?
Narrator	Then he stood up. He sounded a bit annoyed.
Jesus	Quiet! That's enough!
Andrew	What does he mean?
Narrator	The wind and waves began to die down! And the waves got smaller!
All	Phew!
Peter	Now bail out the water, lads.
Narrator	In a few moments it was all calm again. But no one spoke. They loved Jesus.
All	He was their best mate!
Narrator	But a man who could calm a storm with a word? That was something else!
All	Almost scary!

Narrator	They just looked at each other. And Jesus? He just went back to sleep!
Jesus	Wake me up when we get back to shore, lads!

Discussion

The Bible tells us about the life of Jesus. Many of the things he did were difficult for people to understand.
But Jesus had a group of close mates, called the Disciples – they were actually there and saw exactly what Jesus did and what he said.
This story shows how Jesus wanted them to know he was always there for them.
He wanted them to trust him all the time, even when it was tough.
Who's been on a big ship or a ferry?
Has anyone been on a big ship or a ferry when the sea's been really rough? How did it feel? Were you scared?
Jesus was God's Son and he was able to calm the sea and show the Disciples they were safe with him.
What sort of things scare you?
Do you think Jesus can help us when we feel like this?
How can we learn to trust him?

Final thought

Lots of people read the Bible to learn how to live their lives the way God wants us to.
Jesus didn't want the Disciples to be the only people to trust him. He wants us all to trust him and learn from him. He promises he will always be with us and help us to get through any difficult times we have. In this story he was calm when his mates were all panicking.
It's good for us to stay calm when things are difficult, too. We need to remember Jesus is with us.

Prayer

Dear God,
When life is tough and we're scared, help us to stay calm because you still care about us and you're always with us, helping us cope.
For Jesus' sake,
Amen.

Picnic on the Hill

Introduction

Jesus knows that we all need to feel we can help! We feel 'good' when we can help others. He often got people working together to help each other and encouraged them to share with each other. In this story he used a young lad to help thousands of people by sharing his picnic with them. This really was a miracle!

Story

Everyone loves a good story and Jesus' stories were the best.
On one special day the people had come out into the hills from miles around to hear him. It had been a long, hot, thirsty walk and their legs were aching, their feet were blistered. The last stretch was a steep hill. Then they were there! And so was Jesus!
Nobody really minded the walk now – his stories were so brilliant. You could listen to him all day!
And that's just what they did. They sat on the hillside and listened – all morning and all afternoon. The stories he told! They were so funny!
But now it was getting late. The time had flown! It was almost sunset and suddenly everyone was hungry. Really hungry!
Jesus knew they couldn't walk home on empty stomachs.
'Any ideas, boss?' asked Peter.
'Tell them all to sit down,' said Jesus.
'But we've got nothing to give them,' said Andrew. 'We're miles from the nearest shop.'
Jesus just said: 'Trust me.'
Then Andrew led a young boy forward from out of the crowd.
'There's a lad wants a word with you, boss. He's got a packed lunch with him,' he winked.
The boy showed Jesus his pack-up. Five loaves and two little fish.
Jesus smiled and ruffled the young lad's hair.
'Thanks, mate!' he said. 'We'll share them.'
He broke the bread and fish into pieces and said Grace – a prayer to give thanks for food.
'God bless these dinners for all us sinners!'
Then he turned to his friends and said: 'Well, let's get cracking – pass the grub round!'
And that's just what they did. Of course, it took a while, with thousands

of mouths to feed, but it went round. Everyone had enough to eat – from just five loaves and two fish!

It tasted so good and soon everyone was full!

'Now,' said Jesus: 'We'd better clear up. Take these baskets round for the scraps. Can't leave a mess!'

And they collected up 12 baskets of scraps!

Soon everyone was ready for the road.

'See you all again!' called Jesus. 'Take care!'

It had been a day no one would forget. Jesus had given them something to remember – real food for thought.

And they would be back for more.

Drama script

Cast: Narrator, All, A, B, C, D, E, F, G, Peter, Jesus, Andrew, John, James.

This is a pretty straightforward sketch to act out, but the expression on the face of the boy, as Jesus thanks him, is important. The crowd need to show their enjoyment of the food.

Narrator	Everyone loves a good story, and the stories Jesus told were the best. Well, one special day, thousands of people had come from miles around to listen.
All	My legs ache!
A	Blisters? You ain't seen nothing till you've seen these!
All	Ooooh!
Narrator	Finally, they had to climb a steep hill.
All	We're here at last!
Narrator	But nobody really minded because Jesus was there with his stories.
B	I could listen all day.
All	Ssssh!
Narrator	And they did listen – all morning and all afternoon.
C	It's getting late!
D	We've been here all day!
E	The time's flown!
F	My wife'll kill me!
Narrator	They had, indeed, listened all day.
All	Brilliant!
Narrator	But now it was sunset and suddenly they were all . . .
All	. . . very hungry!
G	I could murder a loaf of bread!
Narrator	Jesus knew the people couldn't walk all the way home on empty stomachs.

Peter	Any ideas, boss?
Jesus	Tell them all to sit down.
Andrew	But we've nothing to give them!
John	And we're miles from the nearest shop!
James	There's thousands of people here!
Narrator	But Jesus just said . . .
Jesus	Trust me!
Andrew	There's a young lad here wants a word! He's got a pack-up!
Narrator	Sure enough, a young boy stepped forward. He offered his lunch to Jesus.
Boy	It's only five loaves and a couple of fish, mister.
Narrator	Jesus smiled and ruffled his hair.
Jesus	Cheers, mate!
Narrator	The young boy felt a million miles high. Then Jesus said Grace.
All	God bless these dinners for all us sinners.
Narrator	He broke up the loaves and fishes.
Jesus	Right, lads, let's get cracking.
All	Pass the grub round!
Narrator	And they did. It took a while, of course – there were thousands of mouths to feed! But the food went round!
All	M-m-m!
Jesus	There's plenty more, lads . . . keep passing it round.
Narrator	And the folk kept eating!
All	You said they were hungry!
Narrator	It tasted so good. But at last, everyone was full.
Jesus	Better clear up now – can't leave a mess!
Peter	Pass these baskets round – for the left-overs!
Narrator	And they collected up . . .
All	. . . 12 baskets of scraps!
Narrator	At last everyone was ready for the long walk home.
G	Goodnight, Jesus.
Jesus	See you soon.
H	Have a safe journey.
Jesus	Take care. See you again!
Narrator	It had been quite a day!
All	We'll never forget it!
Narrator	He'd given them something to think about – food for thought!
All	We'll be back!

Discussion

The little boy was really generous when he offered to share his lunch and he was absolutely delighted when Jesus accepted his help and made a fuss of him. He'd got the right idea, all right!

Some people just love the chance to help out!

What do you like to do to help at home or at school?

Does it make you feel good?

Jesus wasn't just showing off when he shared out the food between so many people. He really cared about them and wanted to show them that this is the way to live – sharing with others, just like the little lad had done.

Just imagine what the world would be like if we all did this a bit more!

What can you do to show the people in your class that you really care about them? Is there anything you could share with them?

Prayer

Dear God,
Please help us to learn to share – like Jesus.
Help us to show others we care about them.
For Jesus' sake,
Amen.

Healing Life

Introduction

Jesus' life was spent healing the sick and telling people how they could live the kind of loving, caring lives God plans for us.
Whenever he had the chance to do good, he took it.
He wanted to share God's love with everyone he met and he became well known for healing people.

Story

One day as Jesus was walking down the street, a man called Jairus came up to him, looking very upset.
'It's my little girl, Jesus!' he said. 'She's desperately ill. But I know you could heal her!'
'All right,' said Jesus. 'Lead the way!'
So they all set off for the man's house, followed by the crowds of people who had come to catch a glimpse of Jesus. Everyone was talking about him.
Suddenly Jesus stopped.
'Who touched me?' he asked quietly.
'Don't be crazy, boss!' said Peter. 'Everyone's touching you in this crowd!'
'No,' said Jesus. 'Someone touched me on purpose – I felt power go out of me.'
Then a little hunched-up old lady spoke up.
'Sorry, mister,' she said. 'It was me. I've been ill for so long and I knew you could heal me. That's why I touched you!'
'That's OK,' said Jesus. 'But do you feel better?'
'Oh, yes!' she replied. 'As soon as I touched you I knew I was healed!'
'Good,' said Jesus. 'God bless you!'
As he turned to go on to Jairus' house, a servant arrived with bad news.
'Don't bother Jesus any more, sir!' he said. 'She's gone. Your little girl's passed away.'
Jairus was a well-known man in the town. Everyone knew he was a kind man – no one had a bad word to say about him. They were upset by the news and many of the people began to cry. But Jesus calmed them.
'No! Don't worry! Come on . . . we'll go and see her!'
When they got there the house was full of servants, weeping.
But Jesus cleared them all out and took Jairus and his wife into the child's room.

Sure enough, she was dead. Anyone could see that. But Jesus lifted her up and, suddenly, she opened her eyes.
'Take it easy,' Jesus smiled. 'It's all right. Everything's going to be OK.'
Then he turned to her parents.
'I think she wants something to eat.'
They were over the moon to see her alive again!
'Sir,' said Jairus: 'I can never thank you enough!'
'Don't say anything,' he answered. 'I'm just glad I could help.'

Drama script

Cast: Jesus, Jairus, Wife, Child, Peter, Lady, Crowds.

The actors need to show different moods clearly: worry, sadness, despair, happiness. Keep the crowds small, or the action of the main characters will be lost.

Narrator	Jesus loved to share God's love by healing sick people, and one day, as he was walking down the street, a man called Jairus came up to him.
All	He looks upset!
Jairus	It's my little girl, Jesus! She's desperately ill! But I know you could heal her!
Jesus	All right! Lead the way!
Narrator	So they set off for the man's house. Crowds of people followed them to catch a glimpse of Jesus.
All	Everyone's talking about him!
Narrator	Suddenly Jesus stopped and looked around.
Jesus	Who touched me?
Peter	Don't be crazy, Jesus! Everyone's touching you in this crowd!
Jesus	No! Someone touched me on purpose – I felt power go out of me!
Narrator	Then a little hunched-up old lady spoke up.
Lady	It was me, Jesus. I've been ill for so long and I knew you could heal me.
Jesus	That's OK! But do you feel better?
Lady	Oh, yes! As soon as I touched you I knew I was healed.
Jesus	Good! God bless you!
Narrator	But as he turned to go, a servant arrived with bad news for Jairus.
Servant	Don't bother Jesus any more, sir. She's gone! Your little girl's passed away!
Narrator	Now Jairus was well known in the town. No one had a bad word to say about him.

All	He's a good bloke!
Narrator	They were all gutted by the bad news. Lots of folk began to cry. But Jesus calmed them down.
Jesus	No! Don't worry! Come on – we'll go and see her!
Narrator	When they got to the house, it was full of servants, weeping. But Jesus cleared them all out and took Jairus and his wife into the child's room. Sure enough, she was dead. Anyone could see that. But Jesus lifted her up and, suddenly, she opened her eyes!
Jesus	Take it easy! It's all right. Everything's going to be OK!
Narrator	Then he turned to her parents.
Jesus	I think she wants something to eat.
Narrator	They were over the moon to see her alive again.
Jairus	I can never thank you enough, Jesus!
Jesus	Don't say anything. I was just glad I could help.

Discussion

Jesus loved to heal the sick.
We're not doctors and nurses, so how can we help sick people?
Helping the sick is one way of sharing God's love. Can you think of other kinds of people who may need our help?
What can we do for people who are lonely or worried?

Final thought

Jesus really lived life to the full because he was always there for other people.
Christians believe this is the way God wants us all to live.

Prayer

Dear God,
Please help us to share your love with other people the way Jesus did.
Help us not to let others down. Help us to care for them the way you want us to.
For Jesus' sake,
Amen.

Everything

Introduction

Jesus was a loving and caring person who wasn't impressed by people showing off. He understood when people were really showing their love for God – even if they were poor and couldn't give very much.

Story

The great thing about Jesus was that he always saw things differently. And no one could fool him.

Once he was sitting in the temple, watching how people brought in money to give to God.

Rich people often came in with flashy money bags and tossed them into the collection box with a loud clang, so that everyone noticed what they were doing.

'Look at me!' they seemed to be saying. 'Won't God be pleased with me! I gave loads of dosh!'

However, Jesus wasn't impressed – he could see exactly what they were doing, and why they were doing it!

Were they doing it because they loved God?

No, they were doing it because they wanted everyone to think they were really generous! And to try to impress God, too!

But Jesus knew God doesn't buy that kind of thing.

Then he spotted something else.

An old woman – very poor to judge by her shabby clothes – hobbled in and, very quietly, slipped two tiny coins into the box.

'Did you see that?' asked Jesus. 'She gave more than any of the others.'

'Eh?' Jesus' friends scratched their heads. 'How do you work that out, boss?'

'Well,' said Jesus, 'Those rich folk had plenty of money – they won't miss a bag or two. But that poor old woman gave everything she'd got – that's something really special! And God can see that! That's real giving!'

Drama script

Cast: Narrator, Jesus, Old Lady, Rich Folk.

Most of this story is performed in mime, so expressive actions and faces are needed. The rich folk need to look really proud and smug.

Narrator	The great thing about Jesus was that he always saw things differently.
All	No one could fool him!
Narrator	One day he was sitting in the temple, where people came to worship God. He was watching how folk brought in money to give to God as an offering. Rich people came in with flashy money bags and tossed them in with a loud . . .
All	Clang!
Narrator	They wanted everyone to notice what they were doing. They seemed to be saying . . .
All	. . . Look at me! Won't God be pleased with me! I'm giving loads of dosh!
Narrator	But Jesus wasn't impressed. He could see exactly what they were doing and why they were doing it.
All	Because they loved God?
Jesus	No! They want everyone to think they're really generous. And they want to impress God!
Narrator	But Jesus knew God doesn't buy that kind of thing! Then he spotted something else.
Jesus	Look at that old woman in shabby clothes!
All	She looks poor!
Narrator	An old woman hobbled in and, very quietly, slipped two tiny coins into the box.
Jesus	Did you see that? She gave more than any of the others!
All	Eh? How do you work that out?
Jesus	Well, those rich folk had plenty of money, right?
All	Yes!
Jesus	They won't miss a bag or two?
All	No!
Jesus	But that poor old woman gave everything she had – that's something really special!
All	Everything!
Jesus	And God can see that. That's real giving.

Discussion

Jesus could see that the old lady loved God and was doing her best to show how much she loved him. She couldn't give much but she did give all she had.

How can we show we love God?

Is giving money the only way?

What else can we give?

Final thought

The old lady gave all she had because she loved God and wanted to thank him for her life.

If we love God we need to find ways to say thank you to him.

We need to think carefully about how we can thank him by the kind of lives we lead.

And we can share his love with others in as many ways as we can.

Prayer

Dear God,

Please help us to give our lives back to you – to say thank you for all you have given us.

Help us to share your love with others in as many ways as we can.

For Jesus' sake,

Amen.

Let Him Off!

Introduction

It's so hard to forgive someone when they've really upset you! Perhaps they've called you a name, or spoiled your work, or even stolen something from you. Forgiving them, letting them off, is really hard. It's much easier to hold a grudge and try to find a way to 'get your own back'! But Jesus said it's really important to forgive – to let people off when they've upset you!
It's often said that God can't forgive us if we don't forgive others.

Story

Jesus told stories to teach people about God, like this one.
There was once a rich king. He had a huge kingdom – and I mean huge. It was so big that he had loads of tax collectors – to collect all his money for him.
But one of them was a cheat. He collected all the taxes, but then he spent them on himself. He bought a massive house with loads of servants. He and his wife were dripping with jewellery.
And it all came from the king's money!
But the day came when all the tax collectors had to bring the king his money. Everyone brought the money to the palace – except one. He turned up, but he had nothing to bring.
He was scared – dead scared!
'Sorry, Your Majesty!' he whispered. 'I've spent your money.'
The king was just about to go ballistic, when he suddenly stopped.
'OK,' he said quietly. 'I'll let you off – this time!'
The taxman couldn't believe his ears, and neither could anyone else.
'But don't do it again!' added the king.
The taxman was over the moon.
'Thanks, Your Majesty!' he laughed.
Then he ran out of the palace doing cartwheels!
'Yes!'
Suddenly he bumped into someone who owed him a handful of measly little pennies.
'Where's my money?' he snarled.
'I'll pay you, mate – honest – as soon as I can!' he stammered.
But it was too late! The tax collector was so mad that he called over the soldiers.

'Throw him in prison!' he yelled.

And they marched the poor bloke away. The tax collector smiled a smug smile.

But people gossiped about what had happened and the king soon heard all about it. He was not well pleased.

'Bring him to me!' he ordered, in a voice that shook the palace!

The guards grabbed the tax collector and dragged him off to the king. This time the king was really mad.

'I let you off!' he growled. 'You should have let him off, too! He only owed you a few pennies!'

Now the tax collector was shaking in his shoes. He could hardly speak.

'Sorry, Your Majesty,' he whispered.

But the king was not going to let him off again.

'Throw him in prison!' he bellowed.

He should have learned to be kind – like the king.

God's like that, too – really kind. But he can only be kind to us if we're kind to each other!

So live like that.

Let others off. Be kind. Like God. Got it?

Drama script

Cast: Jesus, Narrator, All, Taxman, Man.

This sketch relies on showing the different emotions and moods of the characters.

We need to see the taxman looking scared as he meets the king, then relieved, then angry with the poor man, then, finally guilty, as he's dragged before the king again.

In his first meeting with the taxman, the king needs to be angry, then calm. He must be furious in the last scene.

The poor man simply has to be very scared.

Narrator	Why did Jesus tell stories?
All	Dunno.
Narrator	To help people learn about God. Like this . . .
Jesus	There was once a rich king. He had a huge kingdom – and I mean huge! It was so big he had loads of tax collectors – to get all the money for him. But one of them was a . . .
All	. . . cheat!
Jesus	Yes, he collected all the taxes, but then he spent them all on . . .
All	. . . HIMSELF!
Jesus	Massive house!

All	Nice!
Jesus	Lots of servants!
All	Cool!
Jesus	He and his wife were dripping with jewellery.
All	Great!
Jesus	But it all came from the king's money!
All	Cheat!
Jesus	But the day came when all the tax collectors had to bring the king his taxes. Everyone brought the money to the palace – except one! He turned up, but he had nothing to bring. He was . . .
All	. . . scared!
Jesus	He was dead scared!
King	Where's my money?
Taxman	I spent it, Your Majesty.
Jesus	The king was just about to go ballistic, when he suddenly stopped.
King	OK. I'll let you off – this time!
Jesus	The taxman couldn't believe his ears.
King	But don't do it again!
Jesus	The taxman was over the moon!
Taxman	Thanks, Your Majesty!
Jesus	Then he ran out of the palace, celebrating.
Taxman	Yes!
Jesus	But then he bumped into someone who owed him a handful of measly pennies.
Taxman	Where's my money?
Jesus	The guy was dead scared.
Man	I'll pay you, mate, honest – as soon as I can!
Jesus	But the tax collector was mad and he called over the soldiers.
Taxman	Throw him in prison!
Jesus	They marched the poor guy away and the tax collector smiled a smug smile. But people gossiped about what had happened.
All	Gossip, gossip, gossip.
Jesus	The king soon heard what had happened and he was not well pleased!
King	Bring him to me!
Jesus	The guards grabbed the tax collector and dragged him off to the palace. The king was really mad!
King	I let you off!
Jesus	The tax collector was trembling in his shoes.
King	I let you off! You should have let him off, too! He only owed you a few pennies!

Jesus	The tax collector could hardly speak.
Taxman	S-s-s-sorry, Your Majesty.
Jesus	But the king was not going to let him off again.
King	Throw him in prison!
All	Ouch!
Narrator	He should've learned to be kind – like the king. God's like that, too – really kind! But he can only be kind to us if we're kind to each other! So live like that. Let others off. Be kind, like God.
All	Got it?

Discussion

Yes, it's really hard to let people off when they've upset you.

What sort of things do you find hardest to let people off?

Is anyone here holding a grudge from something that happened a really long time ago, something you find almost impossible to forgive?

What does it feel like when you forgive someone, or let them off?

Final thought

It's crucial to forgive others – believers who trust in Jesus say that God can't forgive us if we're still holding a grudge.
And once you've forgiven someone you can actually start your relationship all over again – from fresh! What a relief for both of you!
If you want to be like God you have to learn to forgive, because that's the kind of thing God does!

Prayer

Dear God,
Please help us to forgive each other – to let each other off, just as you forgive us.
For Jesus' sake.
Amen.

Sorry!

Introduction

It's the hardest thing in the world to say sorry! Yes, you know you've done something wrong. You know you've upset and hurt the people you love most. You know you need to say sorry. But it's so hard to do it! But if you do say sorry and mean it, people can give you a fresh start – you get a chance to do better. People will forgive you. They'll let you off!

God will never stop forgiving us and loving us. When we say sorry he will give us another chance and will help us to avoid doing the things that leave us needing to say sorry in the first place.

Story

Jesus loved telling stories and people loved to listen. The hours just flew by.

He once told a story about an old farmer and his two sons.

The elder son was a good farmer and worked hard. He never let his father down, but he was . . . boring.

The younger son was a different kettle of fish. He hated the farm and just couldn't wait to get away. He thought he was really . . . cool!

So he asked his dad for his share of the farm, said goodbye and set off for the big city.

In the big city he made lots of friends – they were cool, too. He was always treating them, buying them food and drinks and presents. But I'm afraid they were just using him. So when his money ran out they just told him to get lost!

He had to get a job, and the only one he could get was on a pig farm! Ugh! He hated it, but then he had to eat! He even ended up eating the pigs' food.

Then, one day he had a brainwave.

'I'll go home to Dad!' he thought.

But then he had another thought.

'I don't deserve to be his son any more. I've really made a mess of things!'

It was true – he'd blown loads of his dad's money!

Then he had another idea.

'I'll go home, but I'll just ask my dad for a job! Get some food. Sleep in the barn. It'll be far better than feeding pigs here! I don't deserve to be a son, but I could at least work for him!'

So he set off to walk home. It was a long way! Pretty soon his legs ached and he had very sore feet!

Ah, but what about his dad, you're thinking. Well, his dad had been worrying about his son all this time. He hadn't heard from him. He could have been dead for all his dad knew.

After many days, the son staggered home – thin, tired and starving. And very, very sorry!

All he could say was: 'Sorry, Dad!'

He was expecting a right telling off. But all his dad said was: 'Welcome home, son!'

Yes, his dad was really chuffed to see him. He gave him a big hug and got him some food and clean clothes and even threw a party for him. He was so pleased to see his son again, safe and sound.

Whatever the young lad had done, however much money he'd wasted, he was still . . . his son.

The old farmer never gave up on him and God never gives up on us – whatever we do!

He always goes on loving us!

So, be like the young son. When you've done something wrong, go back and say sorry!

God will understand.

Got it?

Drama script

Cast: Jesus, All, Young Son, Farmer.

The young son needs to begin the play looking very cocky and finish it looking very crestfallen.

The farmer should show disappointment, then, later, he needs to be really excited and happy to see his son.

The friends have to change from being friendly to being stuck-up and hostile.

On his journey home, the son must look exhausted with every step being painful progress.

Narrator Jesus loved telling stories, and people loved listening. The hours just flew by. He once told a story about an old farmer and his two sons.

Jesus There was once an old farmer who had two sons. The elder son was a good farmer and worked hard – he never let his dad down. But he was . . .

All . . . boring!

Jesus But the younger son was a different kettle of fish. He hated the farm and couldn't wait to get away. He thought he was really . . .

All . . . cool!

Jesus So he asked his dad for his share of the farm.

All Now . . . please!

Jesus Then he said: 'Goodbye!'

All See-ya!

Jesus He set off for the big city. He thought he was really . . .

All . . . cool!

Jesus In the big city he made lots of friends.

All They were cool, too!

Jesus He was always treating them – buying them food, drink and presents. But really, they were using him. When his money ran out, they told him to . . .

All . . . get lost!

Jesus So he had to get a job. But the only job he could get was on a pig farm!

All Uuuugh!

Jesus He hated it, but he had to eat! Then, one day, he had a brainwave!

Young son I'll go home to Dad!

Jesus But then he thought,

Young son I don't deserve to be his son any more! I've really made a mess of things!

Jesus It was true – he'd blown loads of his dad's money. Then he had another idea.

Young son I'll go home, but I'll just ask my dad for a job! Get some food. Sleep in the barn. It'll be far better than feeding pigs here. I don't deserve to be his son, but I could at least work for him!

Jesus So he set off to walk home. Ah, but what about his dad? All this time he'd been worrying himself silly about his son. You see, he hadn't heard from him. He could have been dead for all his dad knew. Well, after many days, the young lad staggered home, thin, tired and hungry. And very sorry! All he could say was . . .

Young son Sorry, Dad!

Jesus He was expecting a right telling off, but all his dad said was . . .

Farmer Welcome home, son!

Jesus Yes, his dad was really chuffed to see him.

Farmer Quick, get some clean clothes, and some hot food for my lad! We're gonna have a party and no mistake! I thought he was dead, but he's alive! Yes!

Jesus	You see, whatever the young lad had done, however much money he'd wasted . . .
Farmer	He's still my son!
Jesus	The old farmer never gave up on him and God never gives up on us! So, be like the young son. When you've done something wrong, go back and say . . .
All	Sorry!
Jesus	Good story?
All	Not half!

Discussion

Yes, sorry really is the hardest word. And, of course, you have to mean it.
What's the hardest 'sorry' you've ever had to say?
And how did you feel then?
Have you ever refused to accept an apology? Why?

Final thought

Just occasionally someone will refuse to accept your apology, but God is never like that – he always forgives us and hands us a fresh start. If you can say sorry he won't hold it against you.
That seems a good way to handle life – say sorry and make a clean start again. Just like the old farmer's son.
It sometimes takes real guts to put your hand up and admit you've been wrong!

Prayer

Dear God,
Please help us to say sorry when we've been wrong and made a mess of things. Help us to have the bottle to own up and apologise.
We know you will always forgive us.
For Jesus' sake,
Amen.

Like Your Best Mate

Introduction

Jesus was a Jew who followed God's laws, but people were always trying to trick him into saying the wrong thing, so they could get him into trouble.
One day he was telling people this: 'Love God with all your heart and your mind, as much as you can, and love your neighbours and friends and care about them as much as you care about yourselves.'
'Ah!' said a man in the crowd: 'But who is my neighbour, who do I have to love and care about?'
As usual, Jesus told a story to answer the question.

Story

There was once a merchant up in the big city doing some trading. It was big business – wheeling and dealing. He made loads of money. But he was homesick! He missed his wife and kids and just couldn't wait to get back home. He'd even bought them all presents.
So he set off to walk home to Jericho – that was where they lived. But the road home went through bandit country! Everyone tried to stop him. 'Don't go on your own!' they said. 'Wait until there's some others going your way – there's safety in numbers!'
But did he wait? No, he set off on his own – apart from his donkey.
All the way along the rocky path he kept looking over his shoulder. There were cliffs and big rocks – just the place to get yourself mugged! But so far, so good.
Then, suddenly, bandits appeared from nowhere, yelling and screaming! They threw him on the ground, punching and kicking him.
Then they grabbed his money bags and ran off, laughing. The poor bloke was left lying on the ground. If no one came down that lonely track, he would die.
The hot sun beat down on him as his life-blood ebbed away. Then he heard footsteps. They stopped beside him and he looked up. It was a priest on his way to the temple in Jerusalem.
Now, a priest would stop and help him, wouldn't he?
You'd think so. But this priest just thought: 'I'm not getting blood on my hands!' and walked by.
The sun beat down and the merchant was getting weaker.
Then he heard more footsteps. They stopped and he looked up again. It

was another priest. Surely this one would stop and help, wouldn't he? But this one, also, just thought: 'I'm not getting involved.' And he, too, just walked by.

The unfortunate guy was getting weaker still. Now the sun was beginning to set. It would be dark in a few minutes. No one else would come down the track that day, would they? Then he heard more footsteps. Again they stopped. The guy was now so weak he could hardly raise his head. But when he opened his eyes, he got a real shock. Oh no! It was a Samaritan – one of the enemy! He wasn't in the business of helping, was he?

But that's where he got a surprise! This Samaritan was OK. He bent down and gave him a drink of water. Then he tore up some cloth and bandaged his cuts. Finally, he lifted him on to his own donkey and led him off down the track.

When they came to an inn, the Samaritan lifted him gently down and helped the innkeeper feed him and put him to bed.

In the morning he even paid the innkeeper and told him to look after the poor guy.

So who was the man's real mate?

The first priest?

The other priest?

No, it was the Samaritan.

That's the way God does things. He cares about everyone and he expects us to do the same.

Let's do it. Treat everyone like your best mate! Remember, everyone is your neighbour.

Drama script

Cast: Jesus, All, two or three Bandits, two Priests, Traveller, Samaritan, Innkeeper.

There will need to be plenty of expressive actions and mime in acting out this story. It's quite a straightforward piece, but don't let the robbers get too carried away in the mugging scene – it might be best if they were to do it in slow motion! Jesus acts as narrator.

Jesus	Like to hear a story?
All	Sure!
Jesus	OK. It goes like this. There was once a merchant up in the big city – trading, wheeling and dealing.
All	Big business! Loads of dosh!
Jesus	But he was homesick – he missed his wife and kids!
All	Aah!
Jesus	He couldn't wait to get home. He even bought them all presents. So he set off home back to Jericho – that's where they lived.
All	Oh no!
Jesus	Everyone tried to warn him.
All	Don't do it! Don't go alone! It's bandit country!
Jesus	Everyone told him to wait until there were other travellers.
All	There's safety in numbers!
Jesus	But did he wait?
All	No!
Jesus	He set off alone – he couldn't wait to get back.
All	Trip-trap, trip-trap, trip-trap.
Jesus	All the way down the road he kept looking over his shoulder. There were cliffs and big rocks – just the place to get mugged. But so far, so good. Then, suddenly . . .
Bandits	Aaaargh!
Jesus	Bandits appeared from nowhere. They threw him on the ground, punched him and kicked him. Then they grabbed his money bags and ran off, laughing.
All	Loads of money!
Jesus	The poor guy was left lying on the ground, bleeding to death.
All	He's dying.
Jesus	Yes, if no one came down that lonely track, he would die. The hot sun beat down on him.
All	He's bleeding.
Jesus	Then he heard footsteps. They stopped beside him. He looked up.

All	It's a priest!
Jesus	A priest would stop and help, wouldn't he?
All	Yes!
Jesus	But this priest just thought . . .
Priest 1	I'm not getting blood on my hands!
Jesus	. . . And walked on by.
All	Tough!
Jesus	The sun beat down and the poor merchant was getting weaker.
All	He's dying.
Jesus	Then he heard more footsteps. They stopped and he looked up again. It was another priest. Surely this one would stop and help?
All	Yes.
Jesus	But the priest just thought . . .
Priest 2	I'm not getting involved!
Jesus	This priest just walked by, too. And all this time the unfortunate guy was getting weaker.
All	He's dying.
Jesus	The sun was going down. No one else would come down the lonely track that day, would they? Then he heard more footsteps. They stopped. The poor bloke could hardly lift his head. But when he opened his eyes, he got a real shock.
All	It was a Samaritan – one of the enemy! He wouldn't help, would he?
Jesus	Now that's where you're wrong! He bent down and gave him a drink of water. Then he tore up some cloth and bandaged his cuts. Finally he lifted him up and led him off down the track.
All	Trip-trap, trip-trap, trip-trap.
Jesus	When they came to an inn, the Samaritan lifted the man gently down and helped the innkeeper put him to bed and feed him.
All	Wow!
Jesus	In the morning he paid the innkeeper and told him to . . .
Samaritan	. . . Look after the guy.
Jesus	So, who was the man's real mate? Was it the first priest?
All	No!
Jesus	Was it the other priest?
All	No!
Jesus	It was the Samaritan, wasn't it?
All	Yes!

Jesus	That's the way God does things. He cares about everyone. Let's do it his way! Treat everyone like your best mate! Everyone's your neighbour!

Discussion

Jesus told lots of stories to get us thinking about how we behave. Who do you think these stories were for? Just the people who were actually there, or us as well?
Jesus told us to love God and to love our friends and neighbours.
He wants us to care about them as much as we care about ourselves. That's why he told this story.
In it, one man stopped to help the man who'd been robbed.
How well did they know each other?
Were they friends? Who should we help?

Final thought

Think about the people you meet every day, but maybe you don't really know much at all.
How would you like them to treat you? You'd probably like them to stop and help if you were in some kind of trouble, wouldn't you?

So it would be good to treat other people like that, too. You'd certainly stop to help if it was your best mate in trouble. Well, Jesus wants us to treat everyone like our best mate. He wants us to share God's love with everyone we meet.

Prayer

Dear God,
Please help us to care about the people we meet every day – even those who aren't our special friends.
Help us to help them, even when we don't feel much like it, or when we wish we didn't have to.
Please help us to treat them like our best mates and to share your love with them.
For Jesus' sake,
Amen.

The Greedy Farmer

Introduction

There are some people who actually think that being rich will make them happy.
If you look in the newspapers or watch TV you'll see pictures of lots of famous people. They're probably much richer than you or me. And they often look happy as they smile for the cameras.
But if you read the stories about them, you'll find out that they're often unhappy and lonely people.
As Jesus told us in this story, money and fame don't make you happy!

Story

Jesus often helped to sort out people's arguments – a bit like your teacher, really!
One day a man came up, moaning. 'When my father died,' he said, 'my brother took everything. Tell him to give me my share!'
'No fear! I'm not a judge!' said Jesus. 'But be careful! Don't get greedy – there's more to life than just having things and being rich!'
Then he told one of his stories:
A farmer once had a really great farm. He grew loads of food to sell and soon got really rich.
Then one year he had a bumper harvest – the piles of food he grew were enormous. He just didn't know what to do with it all!
'I know,' he thought, 'I'll pull down all my barns and build bigger ones – mega-big – to store all my crops. I'm rich! I'll never need to work again! I'll just chill out and do what I like for the rest of my life!'
He didn't care about anyone else! He certainly didn't care about God!
But that night God spoke to him.
'You fool! Tonight you are going to die!'
And he did! That same night, he died!
Who got all his riches then? He didn't get to enjoy them!
Jesus said: 'Don't spend your life trying to get rich. It won't make you happy. Give to others who need your help. That's the way to live – God's way!'

Drama script

Cast: Narrator, Jesus, Man, Workers.

We need to see the workers slaving away in the scorching hot sun. The man must come across as arrogant, selfish and cruel.

Narrator	Jesus was always having to sort out people's arguments.
All	A bit like our teacher!
Narrator	One day, a man came up, moaning.
Man	When my father died, my brother took all the money. Tell him to give me my share!
Jesus	Be careful! Don't get greedy! There's more to life than just having things!
Narrator	Then he told another story. It was about a farmer. He had a really great farm. He grew loads of food to sell and soon got really rich.
Farmer	Look at me! I'm really rich and important!
Narrator	One year, his workers worked incredibly hard and he had a bumper harvest – the piles of food were . . .
All	Enormous!
Narrator	He just didn't know what to do with it all. Then he had a brilliant idea.
Farmer	I'll pull down my old barns and build bigger ones – mega big – to store all my crops! I'm so rich now, I'll never need to work again. I can just chill out for the rest of my life!
Narrator	He didn't care about anyone else!
All	He certainly didn't care about God!
Narrator	But that night God spoke to him.
All	You fool! Tonight you are going to die!
Narrator	And he did!
All	Who got all his riches? He didn't get to enjoy them!
Jesus	Don't waste your life trying to get rich! It won't make you happy! Give to others who need your help! That's the way to live!
All	God's way!

Discussion

Who can you think of who is rich and famous?
Are they happy, do you think?
What would make you happy?
Do you know anyone who is poor but happy?
What makes them happy?

Final thought

You can only really be happy if you love God and show his love by caring for others. Nothing else can really satisfy you.

Rich people may look happy in the magazines, as they show us round their flashy houses, but some of them are really sad! They're often quite lonely and feel no one really cares about them. And they often wonder if their friends are true friends or whether they just hang around with them because of all their money.

Jesus loved God and spent his life caring about others. What a great way to live!

Prayer

Dear God,
Please help us to love you and spend our lives finding ways to share your love with others.
For Jesus' sake,
Amen.

Cheat!

Introduction

Jesus really wanted people to love God and get to know him by praying to him. He was really cross when he saw the temple being used as a market place.
He was even angrier when he saw poor people being cheated and overcharged – he hated injustice, and he really cared about the poor people.

Story

When Jesus saw something that was wrong, he got angry – in a big way!
Like the time he went into the temple – the place in Jerusalem where people went to pray to God.
But what a noise! Everywhere there were traders shouting: 'Temple coins! Change your money here! Temple coins! Change your money here!'
This was because if you wanted to buy something in the temple you had to change your money into currency that was used only in the temple.
You might think that seems OK, but the problem was that the money-changers were cheats. They cheated poor people by charging them too much, and most of the people they cheated were not just poor – they were very poor.
And the men who sold sheep and little birds to people, so they could give them to God – well – they were cheats, too.
They also charged the poor people too much – their prices were far too high.
All this made Jesus so angry! It wasn't fair and he just couldn't stand it!
Suddenly he ran forward and untied the sheep. He set them free. People stared in disbelief, wondering what he was doing.
Then he undid the birds' cages. They flew freely around the temple.
Finally, he knocked over the scales and emptied the money-changers' bags all over the floor.
It was chaos!
Sheep running around, bleating. Birds flapping and fluttering everywhere.
Men crawling all over the floor, shouting: 'My money! My money!'
Suddenly they heard Jesus' voice above all the noise, and everyone went quiet.
'God wants you to pray here – not to cheat and steal!' he said.
Everyone stared at him, as if to say: 'Who does he think he is?'

They were angry – mad!
'You'll pay for this!' they shouted back at him.
Jesus had made many enemies that day. But sometimes you just have to do what's right. Sometimes you have to stand up and be counted. That's what Jesus had done that day.
'Remember,' he called over his shoulder as he left: 'Pray – don't cheat!'

Drama script

Cast: Narrator, Jesus, All, Money-changers, Traders, Priests.

The action will have to be carefully handled so that the audience can hear the words and see what is going on.
The person playing Jesus needs to show anger, but also to be calm and dignified. The other characters, in contrast, need to rush about, panicking over their lost money and animals.

Narrator	When Jesus saw something that was wrong, he got angry – in a big way! Like the time he was in the temple – the place people came to worship God.
All	Temple coins! Change your money here! Temple coins! Change your money here!
Narrator	To buy anything in the temple, you had to change your money into Temple money.
All	Right!
Narrator	Yes, that was OK, but the money-changers were cheats.
All	Cheat! Cheat! Cheat!
Narrator	They cheated poor folk by overcharging them.
All	Cheat! Cheat! Cheat!
Narrator	And most of the poor people they cheated were very, very poor.
All	Cheat! Cheat! Cheat!
Narrator	And the men who sold sheep and little birds to people to give to God – they were cheats, too.
All	Cheat! Cheat! Cheat!
Narrator	The prices were far too high.
All	Cheat! Cheat! Cheat!
Narrator	This made Jesus really mad!
Jesus	I can't stand this!
All	It's not fair!
Narrator	Suddenly he ran forward and untied the sheep.
All	Look!
Narrator	He undid the cages and set the birds free!
All	Look!

Narrator	He knocked over the scales and emptied the money bags on the floor.
All	Look!
Narrator	It was chaos! Sheep were running around bleating.
All	My sheep!
Narrator	Birds were flying around, flapping their wings.
All	My birds!
Narrator	Men were scrabbling all over the floor, trying to find their money.
All	My money!
Narrator	Then Jesus shouted . . .
Jesus	God wants you to pray here, not cheat and steal!
Narrator	Everyone stared at him.
All	Who does he think he is?
Narrator	They were angry!
All	You'll pay for this!
Narrator	They were furious!
All	We're your enemies now!
Narrator	Yes, Jesus had made many enemies that day. But sometimes you have to do what's right! Sometimes you have to stand up and be counted! That's what Jesus did that day!
Jesus	Remember – pray, don't cheat!
All	Cheat! Cheat! Cheat!
Narrator	But now he had even more enemies.

Discussion

We often hear about Jesus staying calm when everyone else is panicking, and grown-ups always seem to be telling us: 'Don't get mad!'
But in this story Jesus is really angry. He doesn't lose his temper, but he is really angry about something.
What was it that made him angry?
What sort of things make you cross?
When you see people doing something that's unfair, should you keep quiet about it or tell someone?
Why?

Final thought

If we see people cheating, there are ways we can try to change things. Sometimes when someone's cheating we just don't say anything because we're scared to. But one day it might be us losing out because of cheating. And, more important, like Jesus, we have to stick up for others who aren't as strong as us.
It's really better to say what's going on is wrong.
And cheats have to learn that it's wrong to cheat.

Prayer

Dear God,
Please help us to be brave and stand up for what is right. Help us to look after people who aren't as strong as us and speak up for them.
For Jesus' sake,
Amen.

What a Feast

Introduction

Jesus and his mates were Jews – and to Jews the Passover festival was a very important time. They would want to celebrate together as a family – a bit like we do at Christmas.
But Jesus had some pretty important things to say to his mates.
He had to prepare them for some tough times ahead.

Story

It was the Passover day – a special feast-day for Jews.
Jesus wanted to celebrate with his mates. But they were far from home – in Jerusalem. Where could they all eat together?
Jesus had it all organised – a big, upstairs room. Peter and John were to go there and get it ready – they'd need a lamb to roast, some bread and, of course, some wine – enough for everyone!
So that evening, they all met together for the last time – just Jesus and his closest friends.
Jesus knew that one of them, Judas, was plotting, trying to find a way to give him away to his enemies. And it would happen that very night!
Everyone was hot and dusty – they'd had a busy day! Suddenly, to everyone's surprise, Jesus knelt down in front of them. He took a towel and a bowl of water and, one by one, he began to wash their feet.
Everyone went quiet. What on earth was he doing? He was their teacher, not their servant!
'No, Jesus, you can't wash my feet,' said Peter. 'I should be washing yours!'
'Yes,' said Jesus. 'I've got to do it – I've got to show you something!'
He insisted. 'If you don't let me do this, you won't be one of mine!'
When he'd finished and everyone was clean, he stood up.
'Look,' he said. 'I'm your boss and yet I washed your feet! That's what it's all about, loving and caring! Now it's your turn. Love and care for each other!'
Then he said something that really shook them.
'One of you is going to betray me – to my enemies!'
'Is it me? Is it me?' they all asked.
'It's one of you!' he said.
Just then Judas slipped out into the dark night.
'Now,' said Jesus, and he picked up the bread and broke it into pieces.

Then he gave thanks to God for the meal and said: 'Eat this bread! It's my body – broken for you! Every time you eat it, remember me!'

And he handed it round for them to share.

'And this wine,' he said. 'It's like my blood – shed for you! Drink some now, but every time you drink some, remember me!'

He passed the cup round and they all took a sip.

'You see, I won't be here much longer!'

They all gasped in shock and looked at each other.

'Peter, before the cock crows in the morning, you'll have denied knowing me three times!'

Poor Peter. He looked so hurt. In fact they all looked depressed. Suddenly the happy evening together had all gone wrong.

Jesus wanted to cheer them up.

'I'm not leaving you alone,' he said. 'God's Spirit will be with you! He'll help you! Don't look so worried! And don't be scared! Trust me! I'll never let you down! Whenever the going gets tough, I'll keep you going! Now, follow me, lads – we're going out!'

And they left the cosy little room, and went out into the cold, dark streets. They were scared!

Drama script

Cast: Narrator, Jesus, All, Peter, John.

Narrator	It was Passover day.
All	A special day for Jews!
Narrator	Jesus wanted to celebrate with his mates. But they were far from home – in Jerusalem!
All	Where could they all eat together?
Narrator	Jesus had it all organised – a big upstairs room. Peter and John went to get it ready.
Peter	We'll need a lamb to roast and some bread.
John	And some wine!
All	Enough for everyone!
Narrator	So that evening they all met together – for the last time. Just Jesus and his mates. But he knew that one of them . . .
All	Judas . . .
Narrator	. . . was looking for a way to give him away to his enemies. And it would happen that very night! They were all hot and dusty – it had been a busy day. Suddenly Jesus knelt down in front of them and started to wash their feet! Everyone went silent.
All	What on earth was he doing?
Narrator	He was their king, not a servant!

Peter No, Jesus, you can't wash my feet – I should be washing yours!

Jesus Yes, I've got to do it – I've got to show you something! If you don't let me do it, you won't be one of us!

Narrator When he'd done everyone, he stood up.

Jesus Look, lads, I'm your leader, and yet I washed your feet! That's what life's all about! Loving and caring about each other! Now it's your turn! Love and care for each other!

Narrator Then he said something that really shook them.

Jesus One of you is going to give me away to my enemies!

Narrator They all knew what he meant and started asking . . .

All Is it me? Is it me?

Jesus It's one of you!

Narrator Just then Judas slipped out – out into the dark. Then Jesus picked up the bread and broke it into pieces.

Jesus Now, eat this bread. It's my body – broken for you! Every time you eat it, think of me!

Narrator He handed it round and they all took their share.

Jesus And this wine – it's like my blood – shed for you! Drink some now, but every time you drink some, think of me!

Narrator He passed the cup round and they all took a sip.

Jesus You see, I won't be around much longer.

Narrator They all gasped with shock and looked at each other.

Jesus Peter, before the cock crows in the morning, you'll have denied knowing me three times!

Narrator Poor Peter! He looked so hurt! In fact, they all looked gutted. But Jesus wanted to cheer them up.

Jesus I'm not leaving you alone. God's spirit will be with you! He'll help you! Don't look so worried! And don't be scared! Trust me! I'll never let you down! Whenever the going gets tough, I'll be there for you!

Narrator He looked at their worried faces.

Jesus Now, lads, we're going out.

Narrator And they left the warm, cosy room, and went out into the cold, dark streets. They were so scared!

Discussion

Jesus wanted to show his mates how to care for each other. That's why he knelt down and washed their feet.

Think of some ways that you can care for your friends.
Most bosses expect people to do things for them. But Jesus acted like a servant.
What would a good boss really be like?

Final thought

Jesus wanted his followers to help and care for each other – like he did. God wants us to support and encourage each other just like Jesus did. This way we can be a strong team and share God's love to make the world a better place.

Prayer

Dear God,
Please help us to help each other and care for each other, like Jesus did. Help us to encourage our friends so that we can work together as a strong team to share your love and make the world a better place.
For Jesus' sake,
Amen.

Stay Awake!

Introduction

Jesus' friends – the Disciples – must have been feeling very worried when Jesus told them he wouldn't be with them much longer. The evening that had begun with everyone enjoying a meal together suddenly seemed to have changed.

What did Jesus mean?

He said he wouldn't be with them much longer and that Peter, one of his closest friends, was going to let him down really badly by pretending not to know him!

Everything suddenly seemed to be going wrong.

And now Jesus was taking them out of the safety of the little room, out into the streets of Jerusalem, where his enemies might be waiting for them.

This was certainly going to be a test of their courage. Would they stand by him if they were in danger?

How can you stand by your mates when there's trouble?

How could you let them down?

Story

Jesus was taking the Disciples somewhere. Out of the warm, safe little room where they'd been celebrating together. Out into the dark, narrow streets of Jerusalem. But where were they going?

Then they realised. To the garden – they'd been there before.

A quiet spot outside the city walls.

But it was late and they were all sleepy tonight.

'Stay here,' said Jesus. 'I need to pray.' And he left them, taking Peter, James and John with him. They went over to a quiet spot.

'I'm so lonely,' said Jesus. 'Stay with me, lads!'

He knelt down and started to pray. They could almost hear his words.

'There's a lot of suffering ahead, Father. You can stop it if you want to – but that's up to you! Please help me!'

He was sweating blood.

Jesus looked round, but his mates had given in. They were fast asleep.

He shook them awake.

'Wake up! You need to pray for strength, too – so you don't run away!'

He kept going off to pray. He looked so worried. But every time he came back they were asleep again.

Finally he said: 'Wake up! They've come for me – my enemies – they've got the guards!'
Into the garden came men – with swords glinting in the moonlight. Soldiers! And with them came Judas!
'I'll go and kiss Jesus – you'll see who he is. Take him away!'
Sure enough he came up to Jesus, but before he could hug him, Jesus said: 'What a way to betray me, Judas!'
The guards knew what to do. They grabbed him and dragged him away. But Jesus stopped for a moment. He looked his enemies in the eye.
'You're treating me like a terrorist! Why did you need weapons? You could have taken me peacefully any time you wanted. We didn't need all this. But you wanted to do it at the dead of night. You're ashamed of it, aren't you?'
Now, you'd have thought his mates would stand by him, right? But they just ran away. Jesus was on his own now and the soldiers took him away. But Peter followed to see what would happen to Jesus.

Drama script

Cast: Jesus, Peter, John, Judas, Disciples, Guards.

Jesus needs to look really lonely and frightened, while the Disciples must look sleepy, then scared as they run away.

Narrator	Jesus was taking them somewhere. Out of the warm, safe little room where they'd been celebrating together. Out into the dark, narrow streets of Jerusalem.
All	Where were they going?
Narrator	To the garden – they'd been there before. A quiet spot outside the city walls. But it was late and they were all sleepy.
Jesus	Stay here – I need to pray.
Narrator	Jesus left the others and took Peter and John with him.
Jesus	Come with me. I need you with me tonight.
Narrator	They went over to a quiet place.
Jesus	I'm so lonely tonight, lads. Stay awake with me.
Narrator	He knelt down and started to pray. They could almost hear his words.
Jesus	There's a lot of suffering ahead, Father. You can stop it if you want to – but it's up to you. Please, help me!
Narrator	He was sweating blood! He looked round, but they were fast asleep.
Jesus	Wake up, lads!
Narrator	He shook them awake.
Jesus	You need to pray for strength, too – so you don't run away!

Narrator	He kept going off to pray on his own. He looked so lonely. But they just kept falling asleep. Then he said . . .
Jesus	Wake up!
All	Look!
Jesus	They've come for me – my enemies! They've got the guards!
Narrator	Into the garden came men – with swords glinting in the moonlight. And who was with them?
All	Judas!
Judas	I'll go and kiss Jesus – you'll see who he is! Take him away!
Narrator	Sure enough – he came up to Jesus to hug him.
Jesus	What a way to betray your best mate!
Narrator	The guards knew what to do. They grabbed him and dragged him away. But he stopped for a moment. He looked his enemies in the eye.
Jesus	You're treating me like a terrorist! Why did you need weapons? You could have taken me any time you wanted! We didn't need all this! But you had to do it in the dead of night! You're ashamed of it, aren't you?
Narrator	Now, you'd have thought his mates would stand by him, wouldn't you?
All	But they just ran away!
Narrator	Jesus was on his own now and the soldiers took him away. But Peter followed to see what would happen to Jesus.

Discussion

So Jesus' mates let him down. They were scared and they ran away. He kept warning them, but when it came to the crunch, they let him down.

Do you ever let your friends down when there's trouble?
What sort of trouble might they be in?
How might you let them down?

When you've let someone down, will they ever trust you again?

Final thought

We all need friends we can rely on when everything seems to be going wrong.
A good friend will always be there for you to help you and cheer you up when times are tough.
We need to learn to be good mates.

Prayer

Dear God,
Please help us to learn be good friends.
Help us to stand by our mates and never let them down, even when the going's tough.
For Jesus' sake,
Amen.

Cock Crow

Introduction

Jesus' mates all ran away when he was arrested – all except Peter, his closest friend. He tagged on behind because he knew Jesus was in great danger and he wanted to be around him. Maybe he thought he might be able to help Jesus in some way, or maybe he just had to be near him. Maybe he thought he was a bit stronger than the others, but he soon found out he wasn't!

Story

The soldiers dragged Jesus away to the High Priest's house for a trial.
This was all very dodgy – a trial in the middle of the night?
Someone wanted Jesus out of the way, and quickly – while there were no crowds to see what was going on and to kick up a fuss!
And Jesus' mates? They all ran away – scared!
Except Peter. He followed on behind. He was scared, but he couldn't just leave Jesus alone with these cruel men – he had, at least, to be near him.
They took him away to the yard outside the High Priest's house and surrounded him with guards, ready for the trial.
It was cold, so Peter pulled his cloak up round his neck and went over to the fire. There were servants about and one of them went up to Peter and stared at him.
'You're one of his mates, aren't you? One of Jesus' mates?'
'No!' said Peter. 'I don't know him!'
He was scared, like I said, and he looked quickly away.
Then someone else came over and recognised him.
'You're one of his lot – I've seen you with him!'
Peter was getting jumpy now.
'No! Not me! I don't know him!' he said.
Then, not much later, another man came over. Peter was talking to one of the servants.
'You are one of Jesus' mates – I can tell you're from Galilee by the way you talk!'
Peter was panicking now.
'I'm not!' he yelled. 'I don't know Jesus at all!'
Then he caught sight of Jesus between two guards. Their eyes met across the yard. Peter knew at once that Jesus had heard him. He felt sick with shame.

Then he heard a sound. It was a cock crowing, and he remembered that Jesus had said: 'Before the cock crows you'll deny me three times.'
Peter was gutted. His best friend was facing death and he'd let him down!
He went outside and sobbed and sobbed.

Drama script

Cast: Narrator, All, Jesus, Peter, Guards, three Servants.

Narrator	The soldiers dragged Jesus away to the High Priest's house for a trial. A trial in the middle of the night.
All	Very dodgy!
Narrator	Someone wanted Jesus out of the way!
All	And quickly!
Narrator	While there were no crowds around to ask awkward questions!
All	And Jesus' mates, what did they all do?
Narrator	They ran away – scared! Except Peter – he followed on behind – he was scared, but he couldn't just leave Jesus alone with these cruel men.
Peter	At least I've got to be near him.
Narrator	They took him away to the yard outside the High Priest's house, ready for the trial.
Peter	It's cold!
Narrator	Peter went over to a fire where the servants were keeping warm. One of them came up to Peter and stared at him.
Servant 1	You're one of his mates, aren't you? One of Jesus' mates?
Peter	No! I don't know him!
Narrator	He was scared, like I said, and he looked quickly away. Then someone else came over and recognised him.
Servant 2	You are one of his lot – I've seen you with him!
Narrator	Peter was getting jumpy now.
Peter	No! Not me! I don't know him, I said!
Narrator	A few moments later, another servant came over.
Servant 3	You are one of his mates, whatever you say! I can tell you're from Galilee by the way you talk!
Narrator	Peter was in a real panic now!
Peter	I'm not! I don't know Jesus at all!
Narrator	Then he caught sight of Jesus between two guards. Their eyes met across the yard. He knew at once that Jesus had heard what he'd said. He felt sick with shame. Then he heard a sound.
All	Cock-a-doodle-do-o-o!

Narrator	It was a cock crowing and he remembered what Jesus had said.
All	Before the cock crows, you'll deny me three times!
Narrator	Peter was gutted. His best friend was facing death and he'd let him down! He went outside and sobbed and sobbed!

Discussion

His very best mate! And he let him down!
Has anyone ever let you down like that? Like Peter let Jesus down?
What did they do?
Have you ever forgiven them? Do you trust them now?

Final thought

Yes, it's really hard to trust someone when they've let you down badly!
Jesus did trust Peter and his other friends again. After he died and came back to life, he trusted them to look after each other in difficult and dangerous situations, and these men who ran away went on to become the leaders of the church. Peter was the leader of the Early Church! Some of them, including Peter, were even brave enough to die for Jesus later on!
This was because after he died, Jesus was with them through his Holy Spirit, who gave them special strength. He can give each of us special strength today.

Prayer

Dear God,
Please help us to forgive others when they've let us down – even when it's really hard!
Help us to learn to trust them again and keep on being friends.
For Jesus' sake,
Amen.

In the Dead of the Night

Introduction

Why were Jesus' enemies so desperate to get rid of him? Why did they want the Roman Governor to have him killed?
Maybe it was because Jesus was totally good! Not just in the things he said but also in the way he lived his life! He showed that God is a God of love by the way he lived his life and spent his life helping others by always being there for people who needed his friendship. This showed up his enemies – they were unkind and uncaring. They didn't like this at all! They wanted to get rid of Jesus.
Sometimes it's really hard to do what is right and live the kind of loving way God wants us to live.

Story

They dragged Jesus into the High Priest's house to try him. They had to get things over and done with quickly – at the dead of night, while there were no crowds about to ask awkward questions or stick up for Jesus. Many witnesses came forward to tell stories about what Jesus was supposed to have said or done. The trouble was, their stories were lies and they contradicted each other – and sometimes themselves! Then the High Priest began to get angry.
'Are you God's Son?' he suddenly asked.
Jesus' answer was quiet, but firm. 'I am!'
'That's it!' The High Priest stood up. 'We don't need all these witnesses! He said it himself! He said he was God's Son! Condemned!'
Then everyone turned on Jesus and beat him up. These cowardly men wanted him dead. But they couldn't write his death warrant. Only Pilate could do that – the Roman Governor. So this time they dragged Jesus off to Pilate's house – still at the dead of night.
'He's a troublemaker,' they whined. 'And he says he's a king – your Roman Emperor won't like that, will he?'
But all this time Jesus didn't say a word.
But Pilate wasn't impressed.
'I can't execute him just for that!' he said.
Jesus' enemies were furious. Then someone had a bright idea.
'It's Passover – you always release one prisoner at this time. Let's see who the crowd want!'
Pilate began to feel a bit nervous.

'All right,' he stammered. 'I've got a murderer in my dungeon – Barabbas. We'll ask the people who I should release.'
Turning to the people in the street below, he asked: 'Shall I release the king of the Jews?'
But the priests had fixed it and the crowd yelled back: 'No, we want Barabbas!' They kept on chanting: 'We want Barabbas. We want Barabbas!' Pilate was really scared now. He didn't want trouble.
'Then what shall I do with Jesus?' he asked.
'Crucify him! Crucify him!'
It was all getting out of hand and Pilate was afraid there would be a riot if he didn't give the mob what they wanted. Then he'd be in big trouble with the Emperor.
'All right!' He held up his hand. 'Have it your own way! You can have Jesus crucified, but don't blame me! I wash my hands of the matter!' And taking a bowl of water, he did just that.
And Jesus? He was beaten and dragged away to die.

Drama script

Cast: Jesus, Pilate, Priest, Crowd.

This scene gives plenty of opportunity for the crowd to shout loudly! Any violence must be kept to a bare minimum.

Narrator	They dragged Jesus to the High Priest's house to put him on trial.
Priest	We must get this over and done with quickly – in the dead of night – while there's no crowds of people about to ask awkward questions or stick up for Jesus.
Narrator	Lots of witnesses came forward to tell stories about what Jesus was supposed to have said or done. The trouble was, their stories were lies and they kept contradicting each other – and sometimes themselves.
Priest	We're getting nowhere!
Narrator	The High Priest was getting angry. He suddenly asked . . .
Priest	Are you God's Son?
Narrator	Jesus' answer was quiet, but firm.
Jesus	I am.
Narrator	The High Priest stood up.
Priest	That's it! We don't need any witnesses! He said it himself! He said he was God's son! Condemned!
Narrator	Then everyone turned on Jesus and started to beat him up. These cowardly men wanted him dead, but they couldn't write his death warrant. Only Pilate could do that – the

Roman Governor. So this time he was dragged off to Pilate's house – still in the dead of night.

Crowd He's a troublemaker! He says he's a king. Your Emperor in Rome won't like that, will he?

Narrator But Pilate wasn't impressed.

Pilate I can't execute him just for that!

Narrator Jesus' enemies were furious. But what could they do? Then someone had a bright idea.

Man It's the feast of the Passover – you always release one prisoner at this time. Ask the crowd who they want!

Narrator Pilate began to feel a bit nervous.

Pilate All right. I've got a murderer in my dungeon – Barabbas. We'll ask the people who they want me to release.

Narrator He turned to the people in the crowd outside his house.

Pilate Shall I release the king of the Jews?

Narrator But the priests had fixed it and the crowd yelled back . . .

Crowd No! We want Barabbas! We want Barabbas! We want Barabbas!

Narrator They kept on shouting and Pilate was getting really scared – he didn't want trouble!

Pilate Then what shall I do with Jesus?

Crowd Crucify him! Crucify him! Crucify him!

Narrator It was all getting out of control and Pilate was afraid there'd be a riot if he didn't give the mob what they wanted. He was afraid he'd be in big trouble with his boss – the Roman Emperor. So he gave in.

Pilate All right!

Narrator He held up his hand.

Pilate Have it your own way! You can have Jesus and crucify him. But don't blame me! I wash my hands of the matter!

Narrator Then he got a bowl of water and washed his hands!

Pilate Don't blame me!

Narrator And Jesus? He was dragged away to Golgotha Hill to be crucified.

Discussion

Yes, it's always hard to live the way Jesus showed us – the way of love and caring. Nobody's likely to kill us like they killed Jesus. But, sometimes people laugh at us if we try to live this way. It's hard when they're teasing us!

What things do people say or do to upset you when you're being honest and kind?

What do they say?

Is it hard to take it? Why?

Prayer

Dear God,

Please help us to live your way – the way of love – like Jesus showed us.
Help us to take it when other people laugh at us or make it tough for us.
For Jesus' sake,
Amen.

Bad Friday at Skull Hill

Introduction

Jesus had many enemies and some of his friends let him down just when he needed them most. When his enemies got him arrested and tried and sentenced to death, all his friends got scared and ran away. In his hour of greatest need, he was left alone. The Bible tells us that he died to set us free. So we call the Friday of Easter 'Good Friday'. But to his friends, it must have been a nightmare – the worst day of their lives. To them it must have seemed more like Bad Friday!

Story

The soldiers led Jesus out of the city, taking him to Golgotha. It was a horrible place – people called it Skull Hill.

They made him carry his own cross, even though they'd tortured him and he was worn out.

It wasn't long before he stumbled and fell – it was just too heavy for him.

They should have been ashamed of themselves, making him carry it after all they'd done to him.

'You!' yelled one soldier at a passer-by. 'What's your name?'

'Simon,' the poor man replied. 'Simon from Cyrene.'

'Well, you can carry his cross!' the soldier barked. 'Carry it, or we'll never get there!'

With Simon carrying the cross, they finally got to Skull Hill – that's where they always crucified men.

They laid Jesus on the cross and the soldiers hammered in the nails.

The pain was awful and Jesus was screaming out in pain. But the soldiers just told him to be quiet.

'Do you think we like this job?' one of them snarled.

They tied his feet to the cross and lifted it up. He could hardly breathe.

'He's in a bad way,' the soldier said. 'He won't last long!'

They laughed at this.

'Good! We'll be back in barracks soon! Just in time for dinner!'

They laughed even louder this time.

Jesus was in terrible pain, but they were heartless – they even tossed coins for his clothes.

'Heads, I get his cloak!' said one.

'Tails, I get his sandals!' said another.

They were cruel days and they thought it was funny to torment Jesus.

'Let's give him a drink of water,' said one.
'Better still, let's make it vinegar!' another laughed.
'Are you thirsty, mate? You will be soon!'
Jesus' mother, Mary, came with his friends to be near him one last time.
He looked down at them. He could hardly speak for the pain.
'John,' he whispered. 'My mother is now your mother – look after her!'
Then he muttered: 'Mother . . . John . . . will be your son now.'
They were in tears – all of them, the men as much as the women. But they knew what he meant.
Suddenly it started to go dark – it was really weird. Jesus took one last breath.
'They don't know what they're doing . . . don't blame them . . . it's over.'
His last words. Their best friend was dead. All they could do now was bury him. Or so they thought.

Drama script

Cast: Narrator, All, Centurion, Soldier 1, Soldier 2, Crowd – A, B, C, D, E, F, G, H, I, John, Mary.

Don't emphasise the gruesome details too much! Jesus can wind his arms across a simple wooden cross for the crucifixion. This should support them for this short episode. Put emphasis on the calmness of Jesus and the hopelessness of the disciples. Jesus' love needs to shine through.

Narrator	They called it . . .
All	Skull Hill.
Centurion	Make him carry his own cross!
Narrator	But Jesus was exhausted – worn out by their torture, and he stumbled and fell.
All	Poor man!
Narrator	The cross was too heavy for him.
Centurion	You . . . what's your name?
Simon	Simon . . . Simon from Cyrene.
Centurion	Well, you carry his cross or we'll never get there!
A	About time too! Making him carry a cross in his state – they should have known better!
Narrator	With Simon carrying the cross they got to Skull Hill – they always crucified men there. Jesus was laid on the cross and the soldiers hammered in the nails.
Soldier 1	Pass us that hammer!
Soldier 2	Give us the nails!
Narrator	Jesus cried out in pain.
Centurion	Quiet!

Soldier 1	D'you think we like this job?
Soldier 2	Now, tie his feet together.
Narrator	Jesus was in a bad way. He could hardly breathe.
B	He won't last long!
Centurion	Good! We'll be back in the barracks sooner!
C	Poor bloke!
Narrator	He was in awful pain, but the soldiers were heartless – they even tossed coins for his clothes!
Soldier 1	Heads, you keep his cloak.
Soldier 2	Yes! It's mine!
Soldier 1	Tails, you get his sandals . . . mine!
Narrator	They were cruel days!
D	Is this the man who went round 'saving' others?
E	He'd better save himself now, eh?
F	He looks like he needs a drink.
G	Let's give him vinegar!
All	What a cruel trick!
Narrator	His mother and friends came down to be near him one last time.
Jesus	John . . .
Narrator	He could hardly speak for the pain.
Jesus	My mother is your mother now . . . take care of her!
John	Yes, Jesus.
Jesus	Mother . . . John will be your son now.
Narrator	Mary couldn't reply for tears. But she knew what he meant.
H	Hey, it's getting dark early, isn't it?
I	Something really weird's going on!
Narrator	The sky was going black. Then Jesus gulped one last breath.
Jesus	They . . . don't know what they're . . . doing . . . don't . . . blame . . . them! It's . . . over.
Peter	It's done!
Narrator	Their best mate was dead. All they could do now was bury him. Or so they thought!

Discussion

Jesus was put to death by his enemies, because he tried to be good, loving and kind. He tried to show us what real life is like – the kind of really good life God wants us to lead. The Bible says he gave his life for us, and people who follow Jesus agree with that.

Yes, it takes real courage to face up to what is wrong and try to put it right.

Have you ever been punished for something that you never did? What does it feel like?

Have you ever taken the blame for someone else? Why did you do that?

What would a really good life be like?

Final thought

Good Friday is when Jesus died to change the world. But that means changing our lives, so that we live in a new way, with real love and kindness. He felt it was worth dying to give us a chance to live in this way.

Prayer

Dear God,
Please help us to live in your new life of love and kindness and peace.
Help us to keep trying even when we make mistakes and never give up.
For Jesus' sake.
Amen.

Full of Life

Introduction

Easter is a time of 'new life'. It's the time of year when flowers and blossom appear again after the cold, dead winter. Young animals are born, like the lambs we see in the fields. Birds lay eggs and we watch them hatch. Easter is also the time when we feel the sadness of Jesus' death. But on Easter Sunday we realise that he's alive again and can change our lives and live in us.

Story

Jesus had died two days ago. But to his mates it seemed much longer. They really missed him. But they weren't allowed to visit the grave on a Saturday, the Sabbath, so they had to wait until Sunday. They got up at the crack of dawn on Sunday to go and see where Jesus' body lay.

The women went down to the cave first. They wanted to wash his body and put on sweet-smelling oils. It was the least they could do. It was hardly light when they got there, but the stone door of the cave had been rolled away. They peered inside. His clothes were lying there – but Jesus was gone! John and Peter came running up, out of breath. They bent down and went straight into the cave. Yes, he was gone! But where? What on earth had happened? They looked at each other.

They didn't understand. Confused and sad, they wandered off. Only Mary was left. Then someone came up behind her. She turned quickly.

'Where have you put him?' she asked.

A voice just said: 'Mary.'

Then she saw who it was.

'Jesus,' she said. 'It's you!'

'Of course it's me!' he said. 'Now go and tell the others I'm alive.'

Tell the others? Mary couldn't wait! She was off after them, running with the news.

'He's alive! I've seen him – Jesus!'

Back home they all had breakfast, trying to make sense of what she had told them.

Suddenly Jesus was there, in the middle of them.

'Boss!' said Peter.

'Yes, it's me.' said Jesus. 'I'm alive again. But you need to tell everyone. It's good news. It's really important.'

Then he was gone.

Drama script

Cast: Narrator, All, Mary, Jesus

The clothes lying on the ground are the only props you'll need. You can try making a cave and stone if you have time. But don't use them if you feel they will distract the audience from the real action of the play. You may feel that miming the scene is a better option.

Mary needs to show surprise and happiness when she meets Jesus.

Narrator	Jesus had been dead for two days. But to his mates it seemed much, much longer.
All	We really miss him. We want to see his grave.
Narrator	You see, you weren't allowed to go there on a Saturday – the Sabbath. It was . . .
All	Special.
Narrator	But on the Sunday morning they were all up early.
All	At the crack of dawn.
Narrator	The women went down to the cave – where they'd laid his body.
All	We all miss him so much.
Narrator	They wanted to wash his body and put on sweet-smelling oils.
All	It's the least we can do.
Narrator	It was hardly light when they got there. But they were in for a surprise.
All	It's open!
Mary	Someone's rolled the stone away!
Narrator	When they peered inside, his clothes were there, but . . .
All	He's gone!
Narrator	John and Peter came running up – out of breath – and went straight in.
Peter	He's gone!
John	Where is he? What on earth's happened?
Narrator	They looked at each other. They just didn't understand.
Peter	What shall we do?
Narrator	Confused, they wandered off. Only Mary was left. Then someone came up behind her. She turned round quickly.
Mary	Where have you put him?
Jesus	Mary!
Mary	Jesus, it's you!
Jesus	Of course it's me! Now go and tell the others I'm alive!

Narrator	Tell the others? Mary couldn't wait! She was off after them, running as fast as she could.
Mary	He's alive! I've seen him! Jesus!
Narrator	Back home they were all having breakfast, trying to make sense of the news, when suddenly . . .
All	Jesus! You're here!
Peter	Boss!
Jesus	Yes, it's me! I'm alive again. But you need to tell everyone – it's . . .
All	Good news!
Jesus	Tell everyone! It's important!

Discussion

Christians believe that Jesus is alive. They say he really died on the cross when his enemies had him executed on Good Friday.
But they believe that God brought him back to life on Easter Sunday, when his friends actually saw him alive.
Many people say this is too hard to believe. But Christians say it's true – they know he's alive because he's alive in them!

Does Jesus being alive again make any difference to us and how we should live?

What kind of life does he live in us?
Can he really help us to live in love and kindness and goodness?

What kind of real goodness does Jesus give us?

Prayer

Dear God,
Thank you for the new life you give us.
Please help us to share your love and kindness and goodness with everyone.
For Jesus' sake.
Amen.